WE LOVE 1D

By Sarah Palmer

Pedigree®

Published 2012.

Pedigree Books Limited, Beech Hill House,
Walnut Gardens, Exeter, Devon EX4 4DH

www.pedigreebooks.com | books@pedigreegroup.co.uk

Content and format: this Smash Hits Annual 'Special' is published as an independent tribute, with all included material sourced and openly available in the market for use, and is not published in conjunction with One Direction or their management

All images courtesy of Rex Features

ISBN 9781907602764

NYC
NERF

Harry

Liam

Louis

Niall

Zayn

Contents

WE♥
1D
Harry

FACT FILE

Harry

Full name Harry Edward Styles

DOB 1/2/1994

Nickname Hazza

Height 5ft 10"

From Cheshire

Siblings One older sister, Jemma.

Favourite song Shine on You Crazy Diamond by Pink Floyd.

First ever concert Nickelback.

Superpower he would most like Time travel.

Dislikes: Swearing and olives.

Before 1D Harry was at school and working in a bakery at weekends.

Top grooming product L'Oréal Elvive shampoo.

Fave aftershave Diesel Fuel For Life.

Sleeping attire Nothing!

Random! Harry was the brains behind One Direction's name.

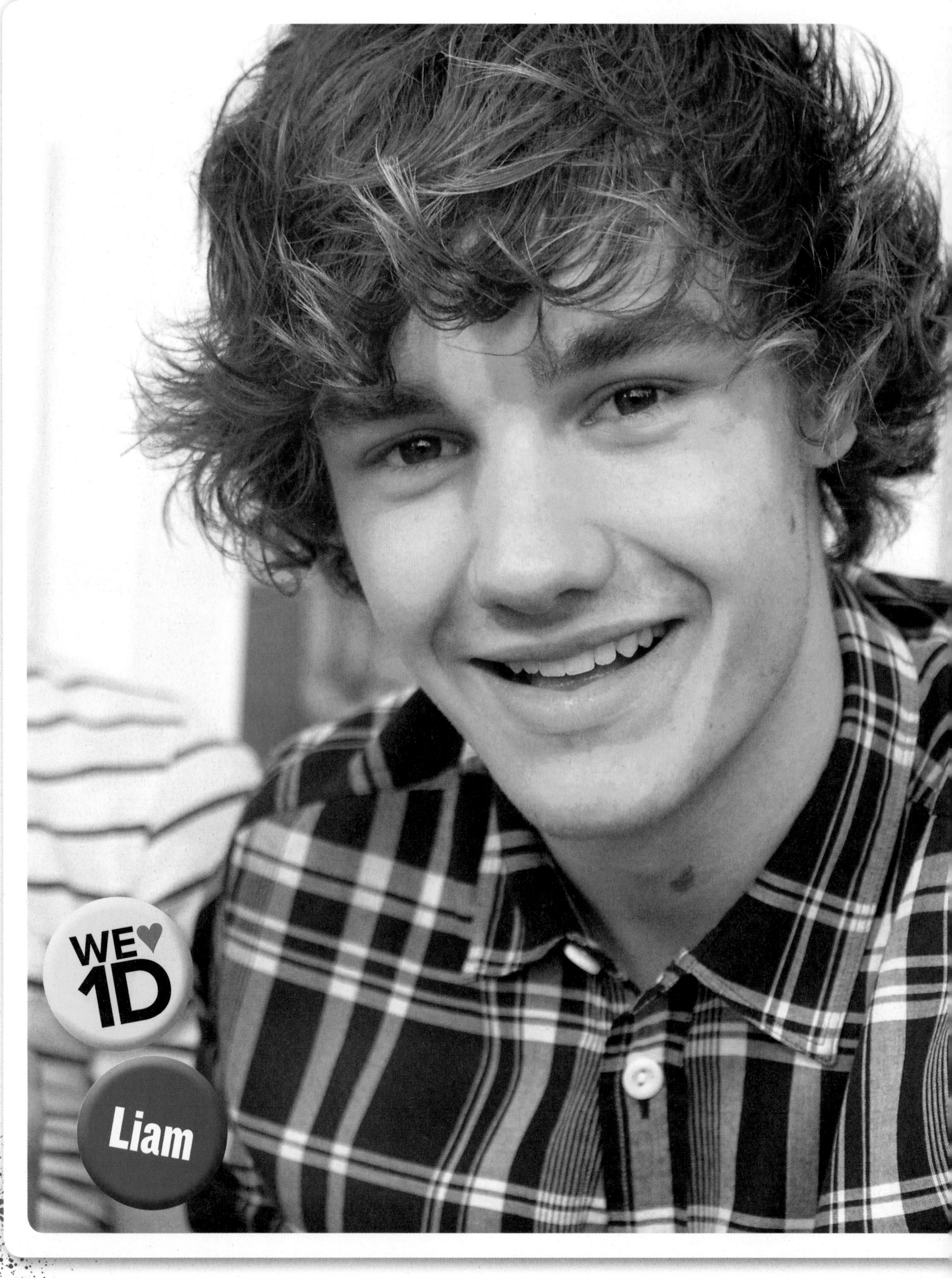
WE ♥ 1D
Liam

FACT FILE

Liam

Full name Liam James Payne

DOB 29/8/1993

Nickname Paynee

Height 5ft 10”

From Wolverhampton

Siblings Two sisters, Nicole and Ruth.

Favourite song Happy Birthday (because it means you get presents!).

First ever concert Gareth Gates.

Superpower he would most like Invisibility.

Dislikes Spoons and flying.

Before 1D Liam was studying and playing loads of gigs.

Top grooming product Hair wax.

Fave aftershave 1 Million by Paco Rabanne.

Sleeping attire Nothing!

Random! Liam’s sisters used to dress him up in girls’ clothes.

WE ♥ 1D
Louis

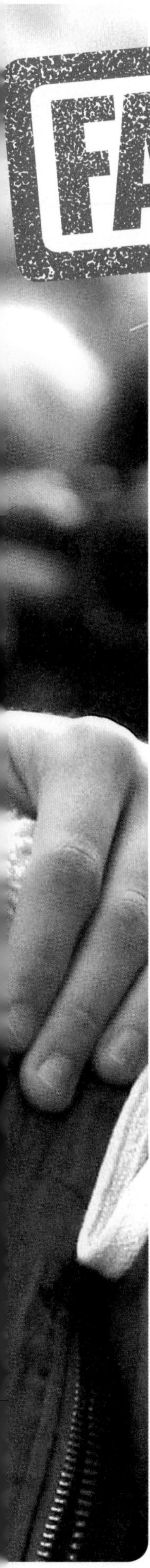

FACT FILE

Louis

Full name Louis William Tomlinson

DOB 24/12/1991

Nickname Lou Boo Bear

Height 5ft 9"

From Doncaster

Siblings Four sisters: Twins Daisy and Phoebe, and Charlotte and Felicite.

Favourite song Look After You by The Fray.

First ever concert Busted

Superpower he would most like To be able to stay young forever.

Dislikes Smoking and baked beans.

Before 1D Louis was at college and working in a cinema.

Top grooming product Dry shampoo, for when he can't be bothered to wash his hair!

Fave aftershave Hollister.

Sleeping attire Pyjama bottoms or nothing!

Random! Louis used to hate shopping but he's now addicted.

WE ♥ 1D
Niall

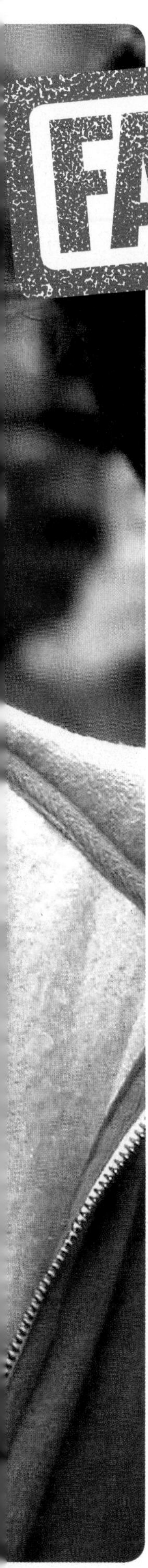

FACT FILE

Niall

Full name Niall James Horan

DOB 13/9/1993

Nickname Nialler

Height 5ft 7"

From Mullingar, Ireland

Siblings One older brother, Greg.

Favourite song Fly Me To The Moon by Frank Sinatra.

First ever concert Busted.

Superpower he would most like To be invisible.

Dislikes Being hungry, clowns.

Before 1D Niall was planning to go to uni and study civil engineering.

Top grooming product L'Oréal Homme wax and clay.

Fave aftershave Mania by Armani.

Sleeping attire Pants.

Random! Niall is left-handed but plays guitar with his right hand.

WE ♥ 1D
Zayn

FACT FILE

Zayn

Full name Zayn Jawaad Malik

DOB 12/1/1993

Nickname Zaynster

Height 5ft 9”

From Bradford

Siblings Three sisters: Doniya, Waliyha, Safaa.

Favourite song Thriller by Michael Jackson.

First ever concert JLS

Superpower he would most like Being able to fly.

Dislikes Pyjamas, sandwich crusts.

Before 1D Zayn was doing his A-Levels and planning to become a drama teacher.

Top grooming product Hair wax

Fave aftershave Unforgivable by Sean John.

Sleeping attire Nothing!

Random! Zayn Googles himself when he’s bored!

Louis is always aiming to please!

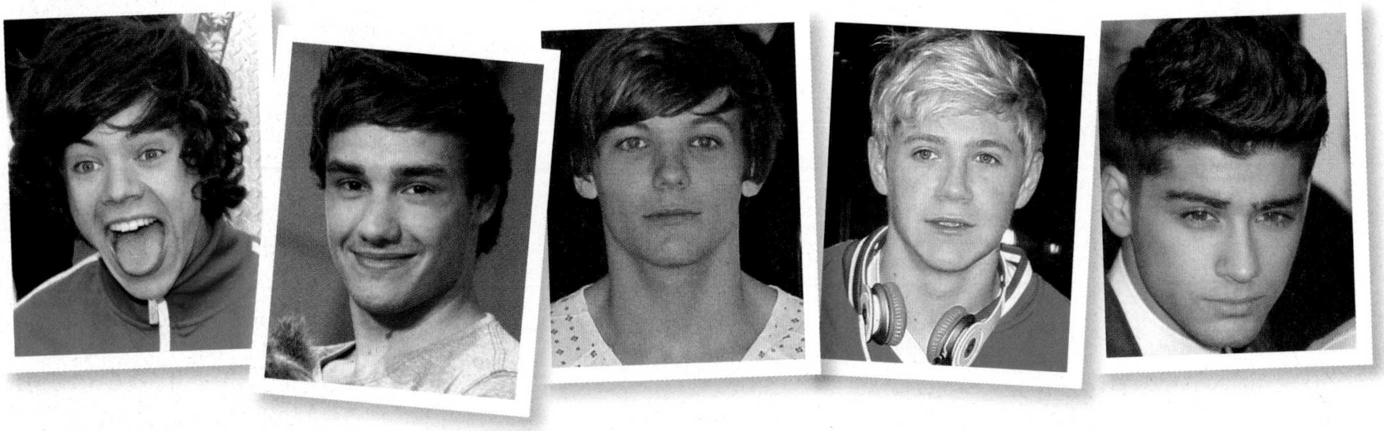

1D's RISE TO FAME

They're the world's biggest boy band, but how did One Direction make it all the way to the top?

In 2010 five lads from the UK and Ireland decided to try their luck on the country's biggest talent show, The X Factor. Louis, Niall, Zayn, Liam and Harry all auditioned separately, but thanks to a twist of fate and some brilliant decisions by the judging panel during bootcamp, they found themselves being put into a band together. And they've never looked back.

They had just five weeks to get to know each other and prepare for Judges' Houses. Their perfomance in front of Simon Cowell and Sinitta would decide whether or not they would make it into the all-important live shows and the chance of winning the coveted £1million record deal.

They all headed to Harry's mum and stepdad's house in Cheshire and practised day and night. They soon found themselves in Marbella singing Natalie Imbruglia's Torn (once Louis had recovered form a nasty sting by a sea urchin!), and thankfully they were picked as one of the four acts to go live!

When the live shows kicked off, they quickly became favourites with the audience, and were saved week after week by the public.

Although they eventually came third behind Matt Cardle and Rebecca Ferguson, they were offered a deal by Cowell's record label Syco and were well and truly on the road to success.

After taking part in the The X Factor tour, they set about working on their debut album, and jetted to LA and Sweden to work with some top producers.

They released their first single, What Makes You Beautiful, in September 2011. It went straight to No.1, and they followed it up with the ballad, Gotta Be You, and their debut album, Up All Night, two months later. Their third single, One Thing, was released in January 2012, and around the same time they headed to America and Australia to try their luck.

By the summer of 2012 they had established themselves as the universe's biggest boy band, and announced their plans for a second album and a world tour. Phew.

In 2013 the lads will embark on a massive tour around North America, Australasia and Europe, wowing fans with both new and old material. Let's hope they pack plenty of Haribo!

Yachts? Sunshine? Yep, it's a hard life being in a boy band

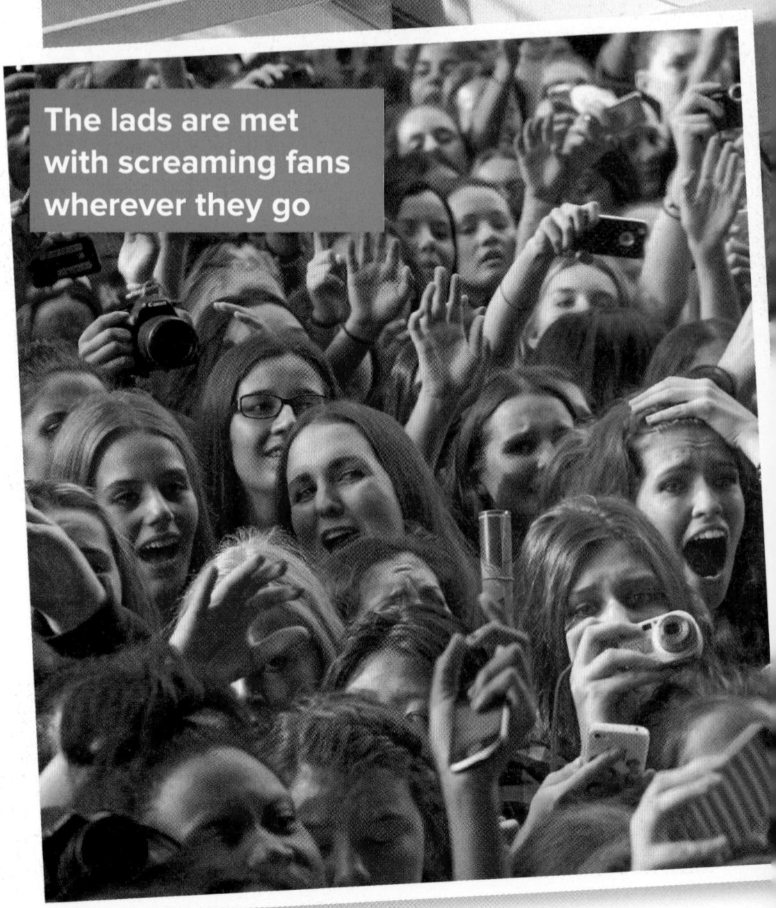
The lads are met with screaming fans wherever they go

The guys hung out at the Men in Black 3 premiere in LA

LIVE!

1

2

3

4

5

1 Put your hands in the air if you love One Direction!

2 Louis sings about his love of messy T-shirts.

3 The boys love to share at their gigs. Mainly cake.

4 Oh Louis, you're ruining the pouting shot.

5 Louis will be furious when he realised his Toms are dirty!

BRIT
BRIT
BRIT
WE ♥ 1D

1D Discography

The boys have already made a huge dent in the charts in the UK. Here are their hits so far. We predict there will be many more to come!

Singles

Heroes (with the X Factor contestants) November 2010 – Number 1

What Makes You Beautiful: September 2011 – Number 1

Gotta Be You: November 2011 – Number 3

Wishing On A Star (with The X Factor contestants): December 2011 – Number 1

One Thing: January 2012 – Number 9

Album

Up All Night: November 2011 – Number 2

1D don't just have huge hits, they win awards! Check out this great collection of gongs they've scooped

4Music Awards

Best Group
Best Breakthrough
Best Video

BRIT Awards

Best British Single for What Makes You Beautiful

DID YOU KNOW?

Want to know 30 ace facts about your favourite band? Read on!

3

1 The boys love eating Haribo before going on stage to perform.

2 Liam only has one kidney because he had one removed when he was a young child due to illness.

3 Niall is a massive fan of Barack Obama and has a life-size model of the US President.

4 Harry once planned to become a lawyer.

5 Liam reckons he's a whizz at making fajitas.

6 Niall likes the idea of trying a bungee jump. Rather him that us!

7 Harry hates rollercoasters – he has a proper fear of them!

8 A fan once asked Liam if they could lick his face. He said no, funnily enough.

9 Zayn didn't own a passport before he was in the band.

10 One Direction's first UK tour sold out in 12 minutes.

11 Niall can make a mean spaghetti bolognaise.

12 Liam once glued someone to their chair at school!

13 Their debut album Up All Night was recorded in Sweden, London and LA.

14 Niall's favourite childhood memory is going to New York for the first time when he was four, to visit his auntie who lives over there.

15 Liam won a swimming race when he was at school. Clever!

16 Liam owns his own pair of pink hair straighteners.

17 A fan once flew 8000 miles from Australia to America so she could catch a

glimpse of the lads at New York airport.

18 The band say they're mostly inspired by Take That.

19 Niall has only ever read one book – To Kill A Mockingbird by Harper Lee.

20 1D's debut album Up All Night was the fastest selling UK debut album in 2011.

21 Liam can beatbox.

22 Zayn has never learnt to swim.

23 Whatever happens, the lads have agreed to have a reunion concert 35 years from now!

24 The boys' music videos have been watched over 70million times on YouTube.

25 A fan once fainted when Zayn waved at her. So would we!

26 Niall used to have two goldfish called Tom and Jerry, but sadly they died after he overfed them. Sniff.

27 Louis once pulled down Niall's trousers while he was queuing for a burger in a crowded restaurant.

28 Niall is the worst farter in the band, and the boys have to open the windows of their car if they're travelling because he smells so bad.

29 Louis reckons he can talk to parrots. Erm...

30 Zayn's dream is to sing on the moon. Well, why not?

TOP QUOTES!

The lads love to talk about, er, everything.
Here are some of our favourite 1D quotes to date!

"We have a choice.
To Live or To Exist."

"I'm very loyal, very faithful, and my mum tells me I'm a romantic."

"I like cute girls."

"I think you have to take me for me. I am who I am."

"I wish I had a girl to cuddle up to at night instead of my pillow."

"I've always wanted to be one of those people who didn't really care what other people thought about them, but I just don't think I am."

"Truth is, I don't mind getting a black eye or broken arm for a girl as long as she's there to kiss it after."

"I like girls who banter with me."

"I'm not very cool. I have to try quite hard."

"We're like the cheeky guys you know from school."

"Being naked is liberating. I feel so free."

"If I could be any person for a day, I'd probably be David Hasselhoff."

"I want to be married and have kids!"

"I don't like really loud girls. I like happy, smiley girls."

"A girl came over to me once, and gave me a hug, then tried to kiss me. I dodged it and then she tried the same thing with Harry. Some girls will squeeze your bum as well, which is a bit forward!"

"I once cried in a restaurant because the waitress told me I could not eat my soup with a fork. I had to use a spoon."

"There's a Hollywood strip where you get all the people dressed up as Superman, and the boys thought it would be funny to put me on there and say I was Justin Bieber."

"I think with our band there's not really the pressure to work out and look good, it's just personal preference or choice."

"My first crush was a girl called Emily and I asked her out by the lockers at school by singing to her and she dumped me the next day. I pressured her into it by singing to her."

"Believe it or not, even when I'm sleeping, I'm dreaming about meeting fans."

Liam

"I smile and I think 'this is my job, this is what I do, and it's all I've ever wanted'."

"I've always preferred having girlfriends to just seeing people."

"Dreams are like stars, you may never touch them, but if you follow them they will lead you to your destiny."

"I'd love to do a Britney and shave my hair one day."

Louis

"I like someone who kind of acts a bit of an idiot!"

"We're not perfect, we're not clean cut. We're trying to be ourselves."

"I wouldn't change anything because I love my life."

"I'm a bit of a joker. I can be a romantic, but not too sickly. I like to keep it on a level."

"Feel free to insult me, but you don't have the right to insult our fans."

"In week one of the X Factor, just to be a little bit quirky, I decided to say that I like girls who eat carrots. Ever since I've had lots and lots and lots of carrots."

"The other day when we were having a picture taken with Simon (*Cowell*), Liam dared me to put my hand on his bum cheek. Simon obviously realised and felt a bit awkward!"

"Live life for the moment because everything else is uncertain."

"I'm not sure there's anything sexy about the way I look. Maybe if I'm talking to someone and trying to chat up a girl, then perhaps I can be a little bit sexy then."

"If you want to go somewhere, you can do. Nothing is stopping you."

"Call me old fashioned, but I like to get to know a girl before I start a relationship."

"I'd like to be Susan Boyle because, you know, she's a good dancer."

"If I got a girlfriend, I'd feed her playfully all of the time."

"I've been looking shabby for the past twelve years."

"I used to have an imaginary friend named Michael."

"My first celebrity crush was J-Lo. Who can resist that bum?"

"I hate it when girls act stupid because they think it's cute. Intelligence is sexy."

"I'm the kind of boy who would fall in love with any girl, because I love with the heart. Not the eyes"

"It's odd that girls ask if they can hug me. Don't ask, do it. I'm just a regular guy"

"Girls? I like someone who can take a bit of banter, and she has to be hot."

"I'd date a fan as long as she didn't scream in my face."

"I can't help but look into the crowd and see if I can see my future wife."

"When I was five I sat in my uncle's wedding cake."

Niall

"People don't appreciate where they come from until they go back. I love going home now."

"I'd rather be a kid and play with paper planes than be a man and play with a woman's heart."

"Fans always ask me to marry them so I'll have a lot of wives."

"I'll always defend the people I love. Even if I'm as scared as baby penguin."

Zayn

"I'm definitely loyal if I've got a girlfriend."

"I find a girl acting cool attractive."

"No matter how many times people try to criticise you, the best revenge is to prove them wrong."

"It doesn't matter how much you flirt the whole day, at night you'll always end up thinking about the one you truly love."

"I like to open doors for girls and that sort of thing, I like to feel as though I'm the protector."

"A girl fainted in front of me the other day. Obviously you don't get to see things like that unless you are The Beatles who have that power, and to see it that close was a bit scary."

"Don't call a girl a flirt, she's just trying to be nice. Don't call a girl obsessed when she's just in love."

"Before you judge people, judge yourself."

"I can be self-conscious – that's why I look in the mirror all the time!"

"Live for who you are and what you want."

"My biggest fear is water because I can't swim."

"Just because you have flaws does not mean you aren't beautiful."

WE ♥
1D

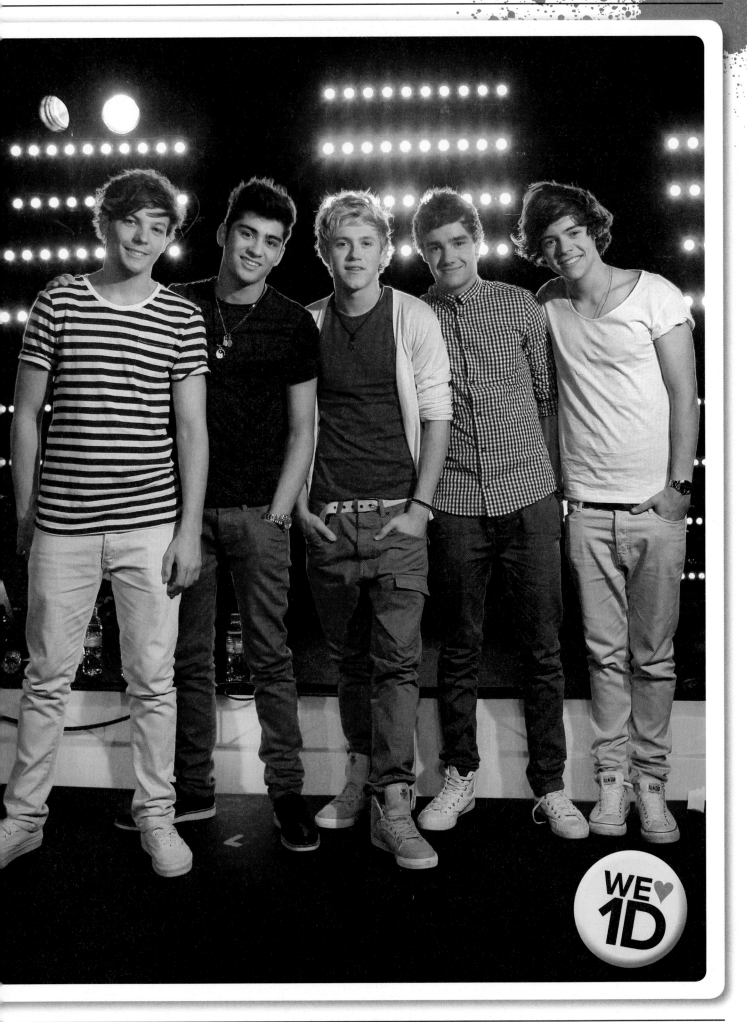

WHY WE LOVE 1D

There are a million reasons to love 1D – here are just some of our favourites

They're kind

Niall once offered to give up his hotel room so some fans could use it because he was worried about them being cold. He also took jumpers out to some girls who had been waiting in the rain to see the band. Sweet!

They're not afraid to show their true feelings

Liam cries at Toy Story 3, and Niall cried at Finding Nemo (he also cried when his mum left him alone on the first day of school). Meanwhile, Louis regularly cries at romantic comedies. Ahhh.

They play good jokes on people

Louis once hacked his girlfriend Eleanor's Twitter account and claimed that she loves Barney the Dinosaur. Shame!

They're lovely to the ladies

Harry says he's glad he's got an older sister because she's taught him how to treat girls right. Niall also thinks that being nice to girls is the best thing a guy can do.

They're touchy-feely

Louis says he's totally fine with fans squeezing his bum, while Niall once went against a security guard's orders and gave a fan a huge hug because she was crying.

They do weird things with food

Harry has admitted that he used to write on toast with food colouring when he was a kid, and Liam likes to eat ice-cream with a fork.

They're 100 per cent best mates and incredibly loyal to each other

They wear matching friendship

bracelets and when they're not together they miss each other so much they text non-stop. Louis also keeps a picture of him and Harry on his bedside table!

They look after each other

When Niall is homesick the other boys talk in an Irish accent to make him feel happier. Zayn also held Harry's hand when he got his first tattoo. That's dedication.

They love their fans

The lads say that one day they'd like to give their fans the chance to star in one of their videos instead of using professional actresses or models. Hurray!

They read your tweets

Liam checks his tweets every morning and loves reading messages from fans because they make his day. The boys also sometimes set up secret Twitter accounts and pretend to be fans so they can chat to people like you!

They have crazy dreams

Harry once dreamed that a rabbit nibbled off his toes, while Zayn dreamed he got chased by Power Rangers. And we all know about Louis' crazy sleepwalking habits...

They're mummy's boys

All the lads are close to their mums, and Harry even runs his ma relaxing baths when he's back home.

They're still amazingly down to earth despite their success

They may be world-famous now, but the boys say they'll never get too big for their boots and will always manage to keep each other grounded when things are going crazy around them.

They never stop laughing

Niall laughed non-stop when Harry walked into a glass door when the band were hanging in LA. The other boys laughed even louder when Niall then walked into the same door himself! Erm, so would we.

FAMOUS FANS

Even the celebs can't help but love One Direction. Check out this amazing array of celeb devotees!

DAPPY He may be a bit dappy, but he's not silly, and he knows talent when he sees it. Dappy said of the guys: "As singers they're just amazing." Yep!

KATY PERRY Katy first met Niall when she was a guest judge on The X Factor, and was partly responsible for him getting through to the next round.

DELTA GOODREM When 1D smashed Oz she said, "It's great to see it in this country when people getting really excited about a band. I love it."

TAYLOR SWIFT Even Taylor isn't immune to the chaps' charms. She was seen dancing along to their performance at the 2012 US Kids' Choice Awards.

DEMI LOVATO The lads met Demi when they were taking America by storm and she later said she loved the band – particularly "adorable" Niall.

JUSTIN BIEBER Harry and co met Justin during their travels around the US and even got to visit his house and hang out.

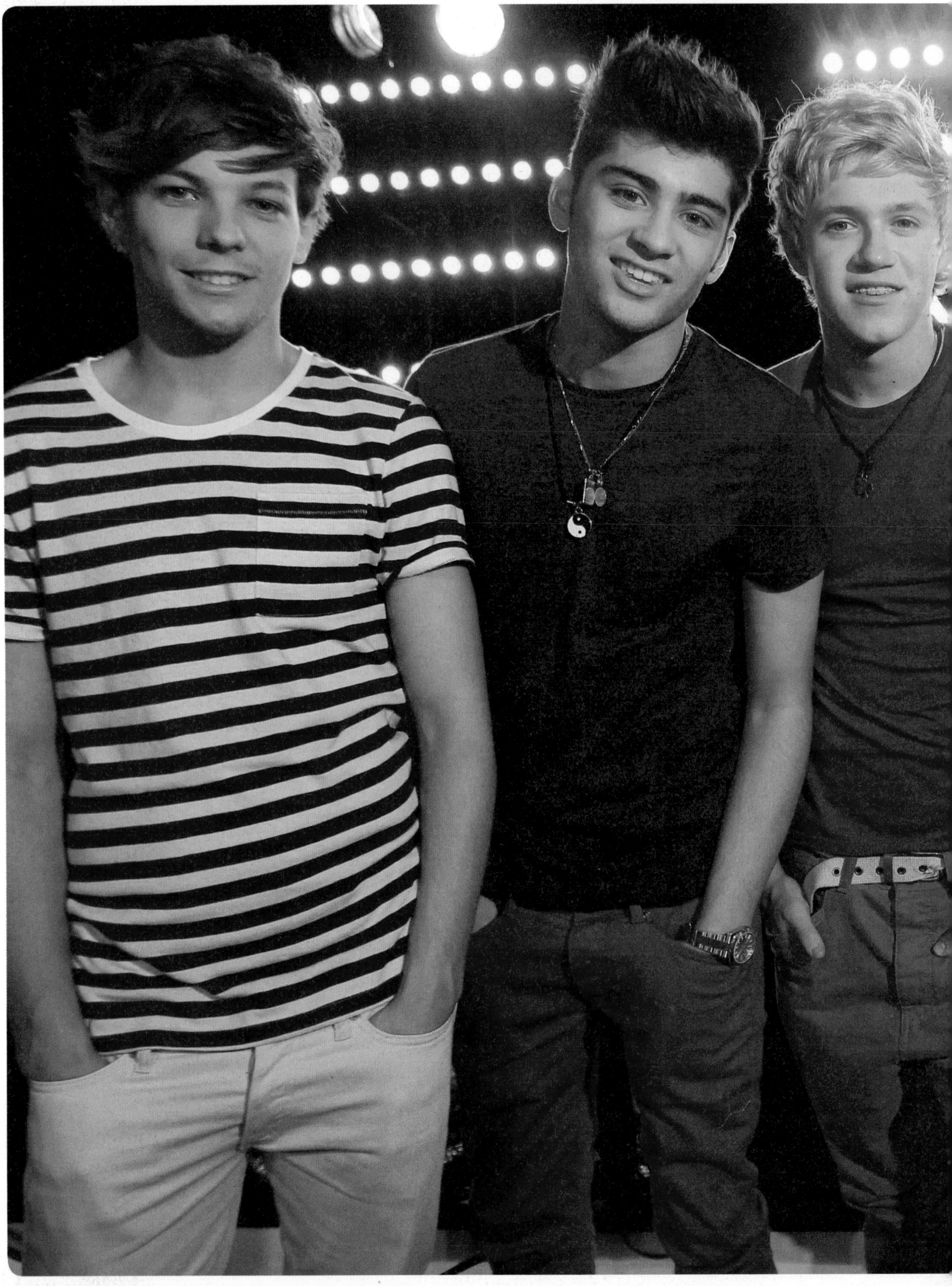

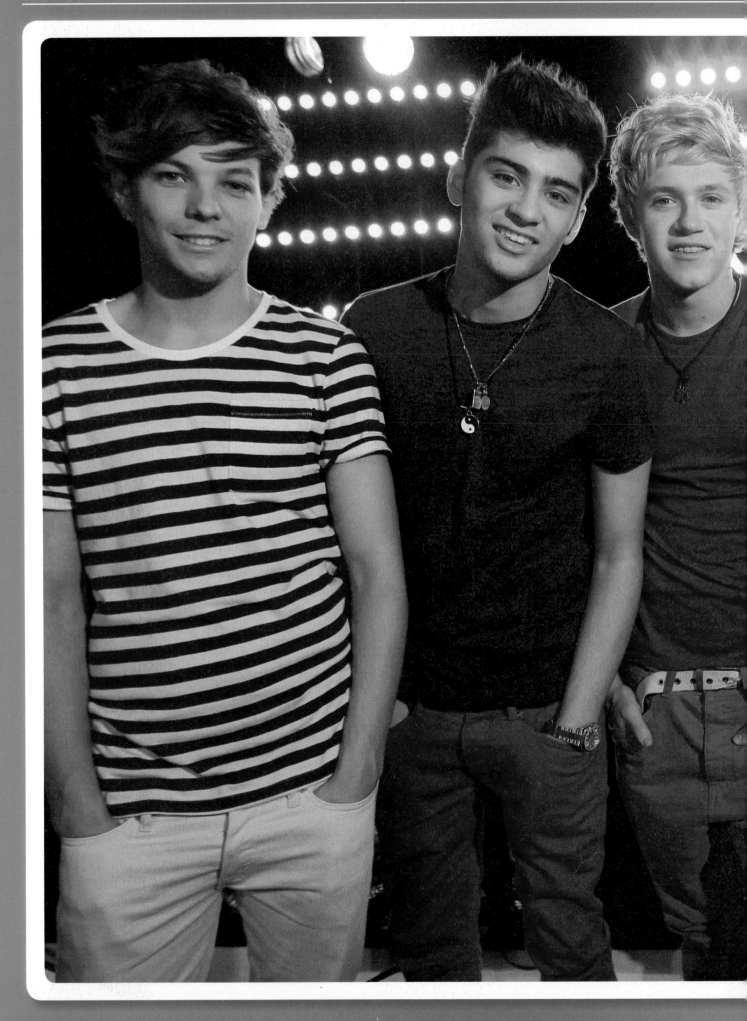

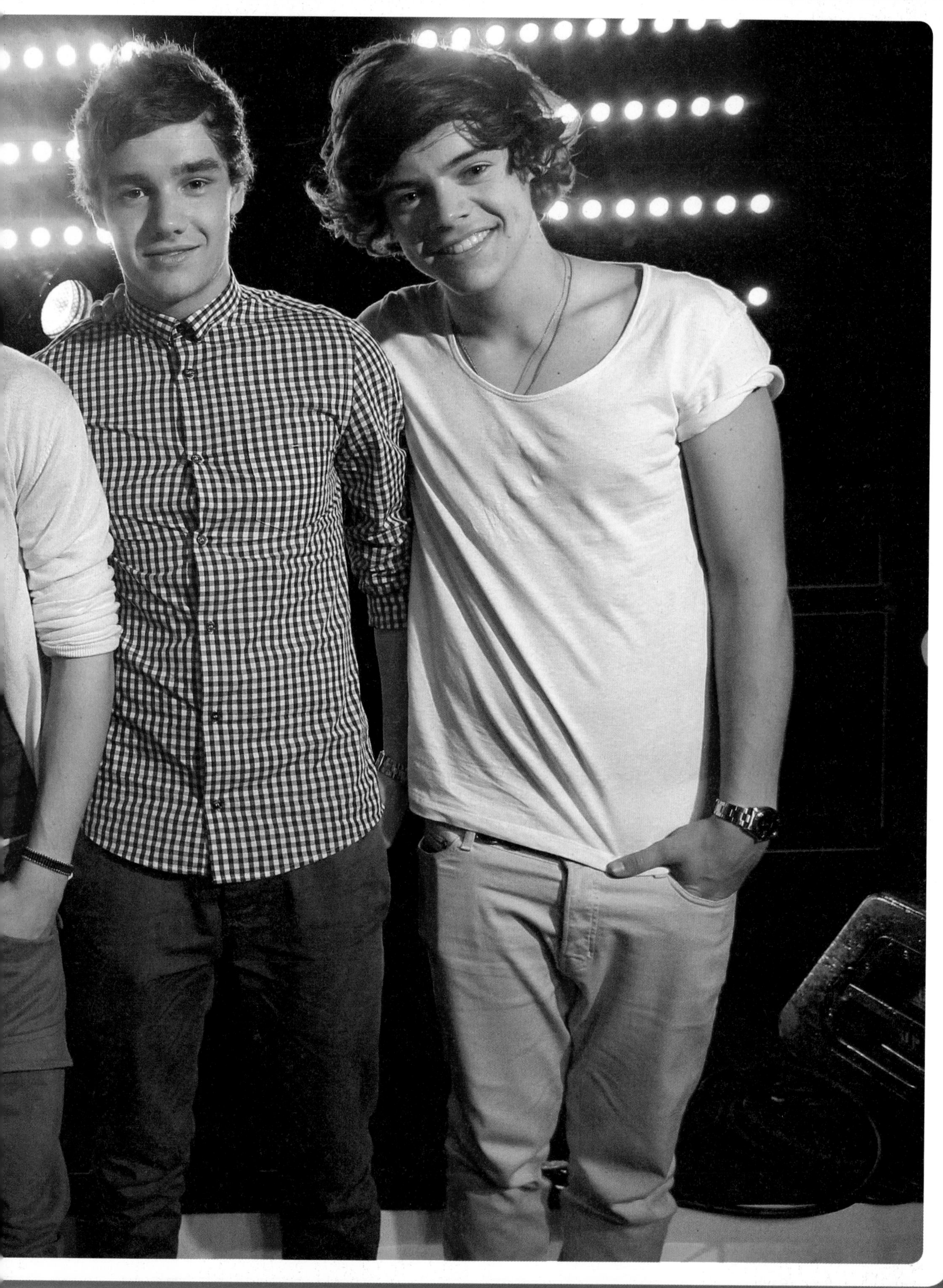

PAPPED!

There's no escape from the limelight when you're in 1D!

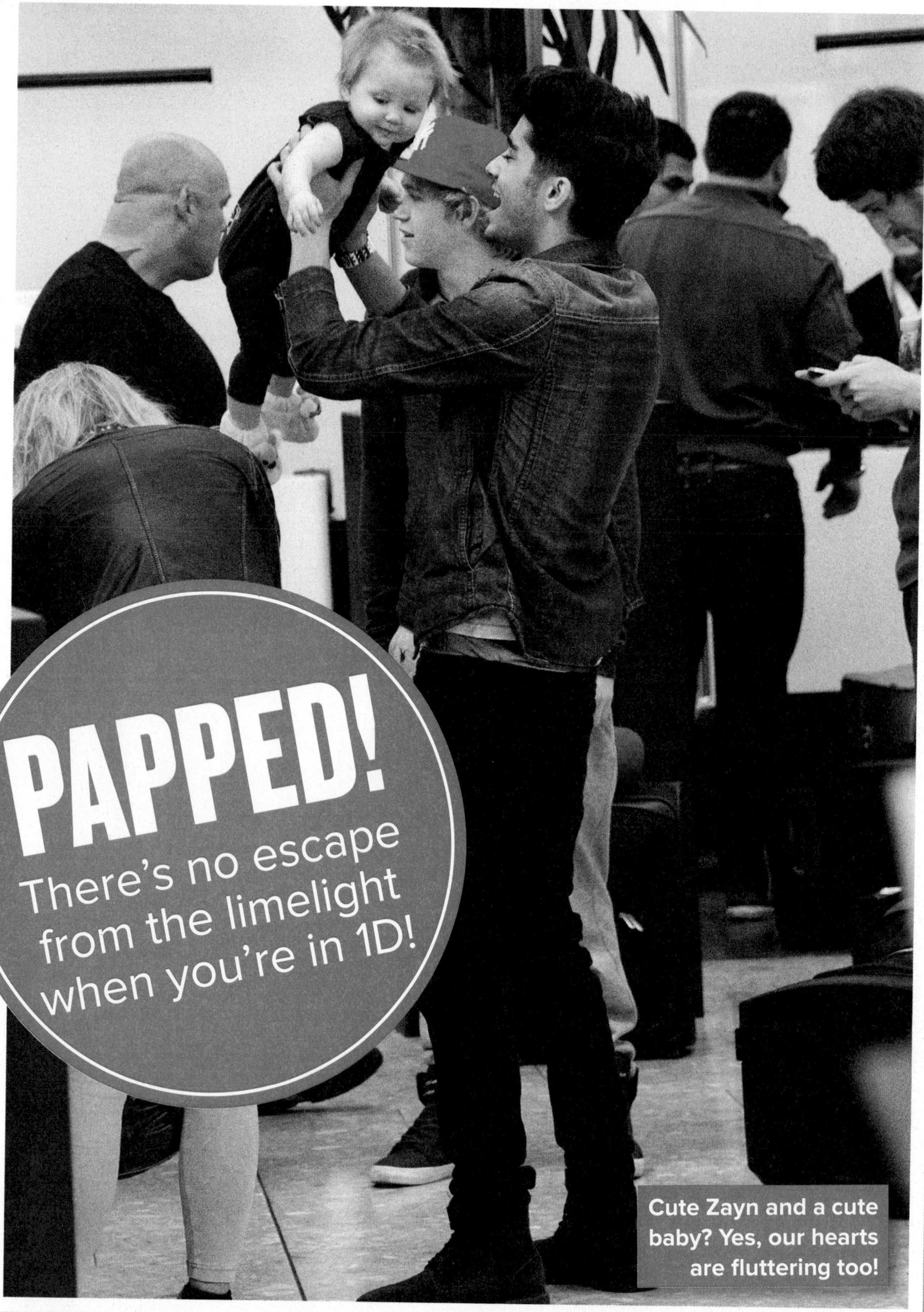

Cute Zayn and a cute baby? Yes, our hearts are fluttering too!

Lounging on boats in Oz? It's a hard life for the lads

Niall is rarely without his trusty guitar

"So many autographs to sign, so little time..."

These Are A Few Of Their

Favourite Things!

What do the lads love most? Chocolate, surfing and Robbie Williams, to name but a few...

Harry

Elvis His dad always used to play his music in the car when he was growing up. He now says that Zayn's stolen Elvis's quiff!

Tapas He loves the Spanish cuisine.

Juggling It's one of Harry's talents, you know!

Love Actually Yes, he really does love the classic rom-com.

Arctic Monkeys Their first album Whatever People Say I Am, That's What I'm Not is his favourite album of all time.

Beef Wellington He adores the British dish and says he's also quite good at making it.

Harry Potter And The Philosopher's Stone It's Harry's fave book ever.

Laser Quest He loves the crazy game.

Family Guy The comedy cartoon makes him wet himself.

His curly hair He reckons he'd cry if anyone straightened it.

Stripping off Harry is known for taking his clothes off a lot!

Liam

Nando's Liam reckons he could live on their spicy chicken wings.

Sexy And I Know It by LMFAO Liam admits that he often listens to the hilarious track.

Surfing Liam and Louis became massive surfing fans while they were in Australia.

Kim Kardashian She's his number one reality TV star.

Boxing Liam used to box as a kid and it's still one of his favourite sports.

Leona Lewis She's his top lady singer and a top crush!

Toy Story Liam loves all three of the massive hit movies featuring Woody, Buzz Lightyear and the gang.

Singing in the shower He admits it's one of his secret habits – we're jealous of his neighbours!

Disney Ever since his first trip to DisneyWorld when he was young he's been a big fan!

Chocolate There's nothing he likes more than a giant bar of the sweet stuff.

Louis

Robbie Williams The Take That star is Louis' biggest inspiration.

Ed Sheeran All of the lads think he's incredible.

Cereal He loves trying out new types when he's travelling the world.

EastEnders He's desperate to make a guest appearance some day.

Emma Watson He's got a bit of a crush on the Harry Potter actress.

Tea And it has to be Yorkshire tea.

Adele Louis just can't stop listening to the London singer's multi-award winning album, 21.

Glasses He loves it when girls wear glasses, whether they're real or fake.

Prank calls He often makes joke calls to Niall when he's bored.

Harry Harry and Louis have a major bromance going on and are best friends.

Misfits He has seen every single episode of the action-packed supernatural TV show.

Niall

Michael Bublé Meeting him was a highlight of Niall's X Factor time – he'd love 1D to record with him.

Galaxy chocolate It's his absolute favourite sweet treat.

His phone He reckons he can't live without it.

One Thing It's Niall and Liam's favourite track on Up All Night.

Milan It's his top city (and Liam's!).

Horror movies He loves scaring himself.

Bon Jovi Niall loves the vintage rockers and their Greatest Hits is his favourite album ever.

Cheryl Cole He's got a huge crush on the former X Factor judge.

Grease It's his fave movie of all time.

White socks. Niall carries around a pair as a good luck charm.

Sleeping. He admits to being the laziest member of the band.

Justin Bieber He went crazy when JB started following him on Twitter.

BUBLE

MILAN

CHERYL

Zayn

Pretzels Zayn adores the American snack.

***NSYNC** They're his number one boy band of all time.

Intelligence He loves clever girls he can have good chats with.

Chris Brown He reckons his music and voice are amazing.

Southern fried chicken Not only does he love it, but he can whip it up in the kitchen like a pro.

Drawing He's an amazingly talented artist.

Justin Timberlake Zayn has a secret man-crush on the superstar.

Megan Fox The actress is at the top of his hot-girl list.

Thriller by Michael Jackson It's his fave single of all time.

The Hunger Games He's hoping for a role in the sequel!

Lovely eyes He says they're the first thing he notices about a girl.

Manchester United Zayn supports the hugely successful football club (as do Louis and Harry!).

STYLE IT

With their on-trend clothes and quirky accessories, Niall and co know just how to avoid bad-clothes days

CHECKED SHIRTS
Ever since their X Factor days the lads have been hanging out in hip checked shirts.

SUITS YOU
If they're going to an important event, the casual look goes out the window in favour of sharp suit jackets and smart trousers.

OUT

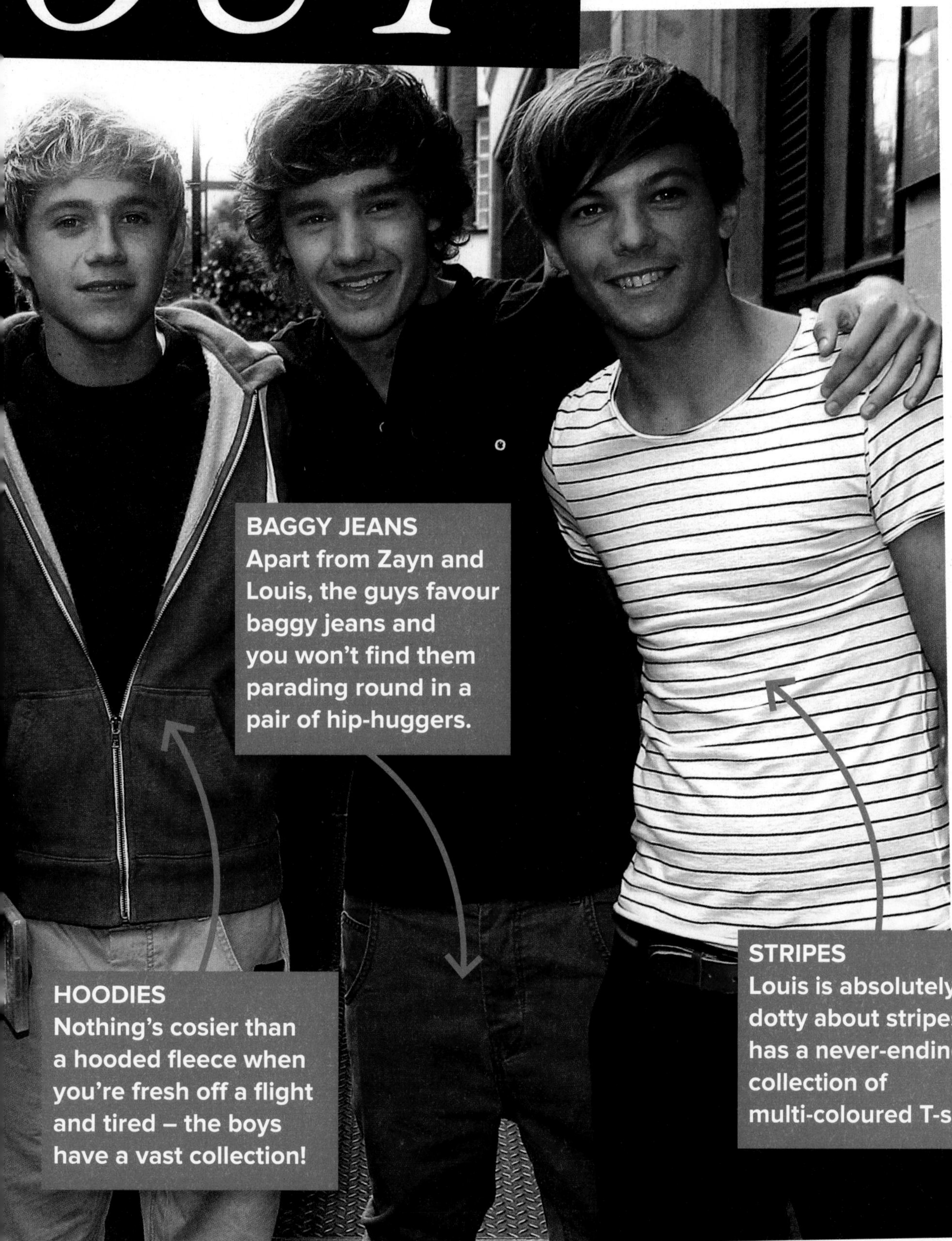

BAGGY JEANS
Apart from Zayn and Louis, the guys favour baggy jeans and you won't find them parading round in a pair of hip-huggers.

HOODIES
Nothing's cosier than a hooded fleece when you're fresh off a flight and tired – the boys have a vast collection!

STRIPES
Louis is absolutely dotty about stripes and has a never-ending collection of multi-coloured T-shirts.

hmv
hmv
hmv
hmv

Spot the difference

Can you spot the five slightly obvious differences between these two pics of the boys?

ANSWERS ON PAGE 77

The super-sized 1D quiz

Think you know everything there is to know about the boys? Test your knowledge here.

1 Which member of 1D was born on Christmas Eve?

2 How is Zayn's name *really* spelt?

3 Who is only member of 1D that doesn't have a sister?

4 What does Louis' girlfriend Eleanor do for a living?

5 What does the tattoo on Zayn's chest spell out in Arabic?

6 Which member of the band sometimes still sleeps with his childhood blanket?

7 Which 1D boy makes a wish at 11.11am each day?

8 Which member of the band did Harry write his first ever autograph to?

9 Who is this? (right)

10 What was Louis' previous band called?

11 Whose half-eaten piece of Vegemite on toast almost sold for AU$100,000?

12 What is the band's stylist's baby called?

13 Which 1D boy wants to swap voices with Niall because his is cooler?

14 Who got attacked by a goat when they were 10?

15 Which band member entered The X Factor in 2008?

16 What shape is the tattoo on Harry's left arm?

17 Which band member loves boxing?

18 What do the boys eat backstage before gigs?

19 Who is the oldest member of the band?

20 Which 1D boy can play the kazoo?

ANSWERS ON PAGE 77

X FACTOR FRIENDS

1D made some great friends on The X Factor – and those friendships have carried on ever since

MATT CARDLE Even though Matt beat 1D to the top spot, it's been said that they see Matt as an older brother type, and the unofficial sixth member of the band.

NICOLE SHERZINGER It was the former Pussycat Doll's idea to put the guys into a band when she was a guest judge on X Factor. She later said, "I'm so pleased for them."

OLLY MURS They may have missed Olly on X Factor by a year, but the guys are top friends now. He says of them, "I look at the guys like five Justin Biebers."

SIMON COWELL The guys have become close to the X Factor king/scariest man in music, and he's called them "smart boys" and claimed they're the future of pop.

REBECCA FERGUSON All of the guys got on well with Rebecca and Zayn later went on to date the glam Liverpool-born star for a while.

AIDEN GRIMSHAW The lads are still in touch with Aiden now and there's been talk of a big reunion at some point. Can we come please?

2012
2012

nickelodeon
KIDS'
CHOICE
AWARDS
2012

IT'S WRITTEN IN THE STARS

We reveal what the boys' star signs say about them, from romance to work to friendships – the lot!

Harry: Aquarius

Element Air **Ruling planet** Uranus **Stone** Amethyst

Aquarians are often great thinkers and are always mulling over the wonders of life, love and everything else. Just like Harry, they make their own rules and don't let others influence how they feel. They are strong-willed, which sometimes means they get into quarrels with other people. Despite that, they make incredible friends because they are loyal and honest and always stand by those closest to them no matter what.

People often see Aquarians as eccentric because they're confident and can be quite crazy at times, and that often spills over into their love lives. They absolutely love being romantic, but not always in a stereotypical sense. If you were to date Harry, you can expect some exciting dates because Aquarians love to experiment and try new things.

Zayn and Louis: Capricorn

Element: Earth **Ruling planet** Saturn **Stone** Garnet

The key thing for Capricorns is ambition. Whatever they do in life they want to be the best they can be, and climb all the way to the top of whatever profession they choose. The important thing is that they have a good balance in life, otherwise work tends to take over and they wind up feeling frustrated and lonely (er, not that we can ever quite imagine Louis and Zayn having that problem!).

Capricorns often have a quirky sense of humour, which people find hilarious and endearing. When it comes to love, they are cautious about getting into a relationship and prefer to get to know the person before they jump in with both feet. When they do settle down, they are fiercely loyal and a great support for their other half, so not surprisingly they're a great catch.

Liam and Niall: Virgo

Element Earth **Ruling planet** Mercury **Stone** Sapphire

Virgos are confident and happy in themselves, but they can be a little sensitive at times. They are also creative and expressive, but they like things to be quite structured so they feel like they're in control.

Virgos love to love, and no matter how many times they get their heart broken, they will always pick themselves back up and try to find the right person for them. Just like Liam and Niall, Virgos are hopelessly romantic and dream of meeting 'the one'. When they do, they put everything into the relationship and do all they can to make the other person happy.

Because Virgos are so sweet-natured, they can be a little naïve and people can take advantage. They need to be careful they don't get walked all over, because they are easily hurt.

1D on 1D!

What have they got to say about each other, hmmm? Lots!

Niall on Louis
"Louis started sleepwalking and got into my bed when we were sharing a room in a hotel. I pushed him on the floor and he sat up, put his arms out and started humming the song from The Jungle Book."

Liam on all the boys
"I'd say in One Direction there are a lot of different dynamics. Some of the boys are jack the lad, whereas I'm a big more of an old romantic."

Louis on Niall
"Niall used to be a jockey. A horse jockey!"

Louis on Liam
"Liam likes to keep in shape the most."

Liam on Niall
"The next girlfriend Niall has must be special. He's waited for you so long."

Liam on the band
"When I was little, I always said that I wanted a brother. Now it's like having four of them."

Liam on Niall
"Liam's bum is like a time bomb."

Harry on Louis
"My first real crush was Louis Tomlinson."

Harry on Niall
"After Niall met Justin Bieber, I had to take him out of the studio so he could scream."

On themselves!
Liam: "I'm the most handsome in the band."

Liam on Niall
"You usually hear Niall before you see him."

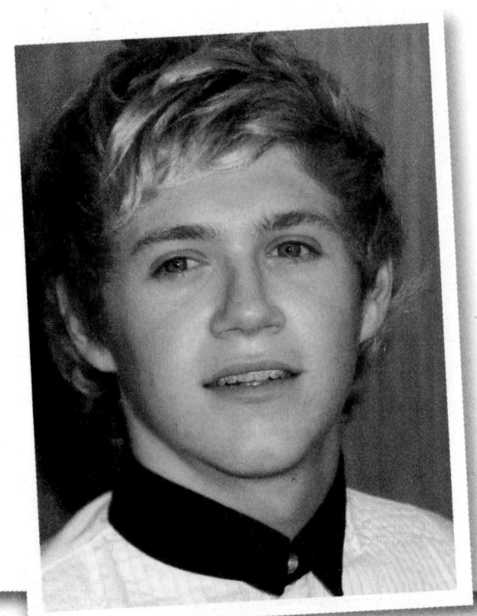

Louis on Niall
"One time, Niall sat on the floor for hours trying to find a way of putting his M&M's in alphabetical order."

Zayn on the band
"I have four boyfriends."

Liam on all the guys
"I found really great friends in these four crazy people. We fight and then make up – there's nothing that can separate us."

Niall on Louis
"Louis has the smelliest feet ever. He wears plimsolls with no socks so his feet get very sweaty and the sweat is captured."

Liam on Zayn
"Zayn hates liars. If you lie to him, it would be hard to earn his trust again. Unless you're me."

Niall on the others
"They're the four best friends that anyone could have!"

Zayn on the boys
"Liam, Harry, Niall and Louis are my brothers from another mother.

Liam on Niall
"Niall's like my girlfriend. Everytime we hang out, I buy him food whenever he is hungry and take him wherever he wants."

Harry on Niall
"The other day, Niall was trying to sing What Makes You Beautiful in Spanish. I stared at him like a dummy cos he did it very well."

Harry on Louis
"Until I find the perfect girl, I have Louis."

Louis on Zayn
"One time, Niall took Zayn's place in front of the mirror, so Zayn started crying and didn't stop until Niall moved."

Harry on Niall
"Niall is the perfect prank target."

WIDE OPEN
3D MOVIE

I Love One Direction Because...

Write down your favourite 1D facts and fun stuff here!

I love One Direction because...

I first started liking them when I saw them...

My favourite member of 1D is...

I think .... is the best singer

My favourite 1D song is...

If I could spend a whole day with 1D I would...

If I saw the boys in the street I would...

If I could give the guys any present, it would be...

The funniest fact I know about the lads is...

If I got to go out on a date with one of the guys, it would be...

The 1D boy who is most like me is...

I couldn't believe it when I found that out that 1D...

I would make a great pop star because...

I really hope that in the future One Direction...

E WRUNG
UT TOO
TIMES

Quiz Answers

Are you a One Direction superfan or a superflop? Find out how well you did in our 1D quiz!

The super-sized 1D quiz

1 Louis
2 Zain
3 Niall
4 Eleanor is a model
5 His granddad's name
6 Harry
7 Liam
8 Louis
9 Harry
10 The Rogue
11 Niall's
12 Lux
13 Zayn
14 Harry
15 Liam
16 A star
17 Liam
18 Haribo sweets
19 Louis
20 Harry

Spot the difference

1 Niall's got a nice new badge
2 Zayn's got shorter sideburns
3 Louis' braces have changed colour
4 Liam's buttons have disappeared
5 Harry's pocket scarf has done a runner